· THE BRIDE'S BIBLE ·

Presented to

_____

By _____

On the Occasion of Her Celebration of
the Sacrament of Marriage with

_____

On _____

·THE BRIDE'S BIBLE·

CATHOLIC EDITION

AVA MARIA PRESS, INC.
Notre Dame, Indiana

Editors Lara Maiklem, Nichola Thomasson

Designer Sarah Crouch

Senior Managing editor Anna Kruger

Deputy art director Tina Vaughan

Picture researcher Christine Rista

Production controller David Proffit

DTP Designer Robert Campbell

First American edition 1999
2 4 6 8 10 9 7 5 3 1

Published in the United States by Ave Maria Press, Inc.,
PO Box 428, Notre Dame, IN 46556
Copyright © 1999 Dorling Kindersley Limited, London

ISBN 0–87793–686–2
Color reproduction in Italy by GRB
Manufactured in China by Imago

· CONTENTS ·

JESSICA HAYLLAR
FRESH FROM THE ALTAR

· INTRODUCTION ·

od, who is love, created you out of love
and calls you to love. The mutual love of a
woman and a man in marriage is indeed an image of
the unfailing love of God. For this reason Christ himself
established marriage as a sacrament and calls you to
make him the center and source of your union.

Just as God has joined you together, God will support
and sustain you in your married life, especially through
the guidance and comfort of his Word. The Bride's Bible,
then, is more than a lovely gift or a treasured keepsake.
It is a guidebook filled with the wisdom of the scripture,
which will help direct and preserve your marriage in the
months and years ahead.

Marriage is, indeed, a holy mystery and a symbol of
Christ's love. As you embark on the wonderful journey
of life together, turn to him often and allow his Holy
Spirit to be your ultimate source of guidance, peace,
and assurance.

MARRIAGE

WE HAVE NOT MADE
OURSELVES; WE ARE THE
GIFT OF THE LIVING GOD
TO ONE ANOTHER.

Reine Duell Bethany

ALBERT-AUGUSTE FOURIE
THE WEDDING MEAL AT YPORT

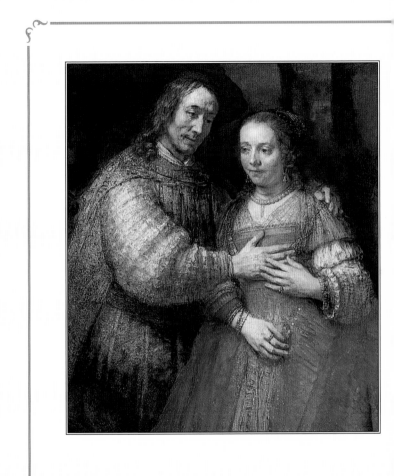

REMBRANDT
THE JEWISH BRIDE

· ONE FLESH ·

he LORD God said,
"It is not good for the man to be alone. I will make a helper suitable for him."

So the LORD God caused the man to fall into a deep sleep; and while he was sleeping, he took one of the man's ribs and closed up the place with flesh.

Then the LORD God made a woman from the rib he had taken out of the man, and he brought her to the man.

The man said,
"This is now bone of my bones and flesh of my flesh; she shall be called 'woman', for she was taken out of man."

For this reason a man will leave his father and mother and be united to his wife, and they will become one flesh.

GENESIS 2:18, 21–24 (NIV)

MICHAEL FREDERICK HALLIDAY
THE MEASURE FOR THE WEDDING RING

· JOINED TOGETHER ·

Have you not read that
He who made them at the beginning "made
them male and female,"

and said, "For this reason a man shall leave his father
and mother and be joined to his wife, and the two shall
become one flesh?"

So then, they are no longer two but one flesh. Therefore
what God has joined together, let not man separate."

So husbands ought to love their own wives as their own
bodies; he who loves his wife loves himself. For no one ever
hated his own flesh, but nourishes and cherishes it, just
as the Lord does the church.

MATTHEW 19:4–6; EPHESIANS 5:28–29 (NKJV)

JAN VAN EYCK
THE PORTRAIT OF GIOVANNI AND HIS WIFE GIOVANNA CENAMI

· AN EXCELLENT WIFE ·

An excellent wife, who can find? For her worth is far above jewels. The heart of her husband trusts in her, and he will have no lack of gain. She does him good and not evil all the days of her life.

Strength and dignity are her clothing,
and she smiles at the future.
She opens her mouth in wisdom, and the teaching of
kindness is on her tongue.
She looks well to the ways of her household, and does not
eat the bread of idleness.

Her children rise up and bless her; her husband also, and he praises her saying: "Many daughters have done nobly, but you excel them all."

PROVERBS 31:10–11, 25–29 (NASB)

SIR EDWARD BURNE-JONES
ARIANE

· A GIFT FROM GOD ·

〜◦)I(◦〜

good wife is the crown of her husband.

House and riches are the
inheritance of fathers:
and a prudent wife is from the LORD.

Charm is deceitful and beauty is passing, but a woman who
fears the LORD, she shall be praised.

A wise woman builds her house; a foolish woman tears
hers down with her own hands.

Nevertheless, in the LORD woman is not independent of
man or man independent of woman. For just as woman
came from man, so man comes through woman;
but all things come from God.

PROVERBS 12:4 (NRSV), 19:14 (KJV), 31:30 (NASB), 14:1 (NLT);
1 CORINTHIANS 11:11–12 (NRSV)

ARTHUR HUGHES
THE GUARDED BOWER

· TWO BECOME ONE ·

ach man should have his own wife, and each woman should have her own husband.

The husband should not deprive his wife of sexual intimacy, which is her right as a married woman, nor should the wife deprive her husband.

The wife gives authority over her body to her husband, and the husband also gives authority over his body to his wife.

So do not deprive each other of sexual relations. The only exception to this rule would be the agreement of both husband and wife to refrain from sexual intimacy for a limited time, so that they can give themselves more completely to prayer.

1 CORINTHIANS 7:2–5 (NLT)

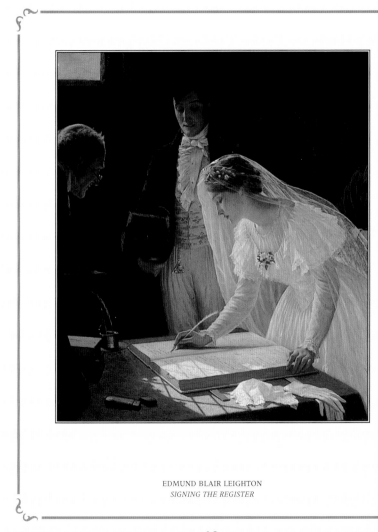

EDMUND BLAIR LEIGHTON
SIGNING THE REGISTER

· TENDER REVERENCE ·

～)(〜

lways give thanks for everything to God the Father in the name of our Lord Jesus Christ. And submit to one another out of reverence for Christ.

You wives will submit to your husbands as you do to the Lord. For a husband is the head of his wife as Christ is the head of his body, the church; he gave his life to be her Savior.

As the church submits to Christ, so you wives must submit to your husbands in everything. And you husbands must love your wives with the same love Christ showed the church.

EPHESIANS 5:22–25 (NLT)

J. SHAW COMPTON
NONE BUT THE BRAVE DESERVE THE FAIR

· LIFELONG FAITHFULNESS ·

Let the word of Christ richly dwell within you, with all wisdom teaching and admonishing one another with psalms and hymns and spiritual songs, singing with thankfulness in your hearts to God.

Whatever you do in word or deed, do all in the name of the Lord Jesus, giving thanks through Him to God the Father.

Wives, be subject to your husbands, as is fitting in the Lord.

Husbands, love your wives and do not be embittered against them.

Give honor to marriage, and remain faithful to one another in marriage. God will surely judge people who are immoral and those who commit adultery.

COLOSSIANS 3:16–19 (NASB); HEBREWS 13:4 (NLT)

DANTE GABRIEL ROSSETTI
REVERIE

· INNER BEAUTY ·

Don't be concerned about the outward beauty that depends on fancy hairstyles, expensive jewelry, or beautiful clothes. You should be known for the beauty that comes from within, the unfading beauty of a gentle and quiet spirit, which is so precious to God. That is the way the holy women of old made themselves beautiful.

Finally, all of you should be of one mind, full of sympathy toward each other, loving one another with tender hearts and humble minds.

1 PETER 3:3–5, 8 (NLT)

LOVE

LOVE DOES NOT CONSIST
IN GAZING AT EACH
OTHER BUT IN LOOKING
OUTWARD TOGETHER IN
THE SAME DIRECTION.

*Antoine de
Saint-Exupery*

WILLIAM DYCE
FRANCESCA DA RIMINI

PAL SZINYEI MERSE
THE LOVERS

· UNFAILING LOVE ·

Love suffers long and is kind; love does not envy; love does not parade itself, is not puffed up;

does not behave rudely, does not seek its own, is not provoked, thinks no evil;

does not rejoice in iniquity, but rejoices in the truth; bears all things, believes all things, hopes all things, endures all things.

Love never fails.

And now abide faith, hope, love, these three; but the greatest of these is love.

1 CORINTHIANS 13:4–8, 13 (NKJV)

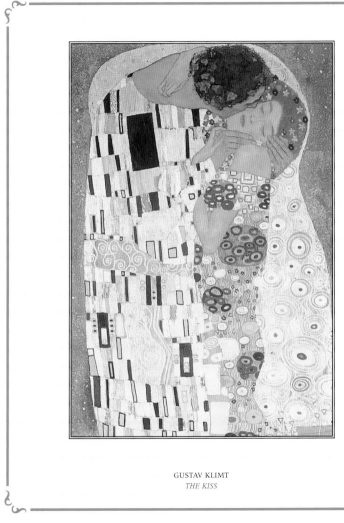

GUSTAV KLIMT
THE KISS

· THE WEDDING SONG ·

his is Solomon's song of songs, more wonderful
than any other.

Young Woman:
"Kiss me again and again, for your love is sweeter
than wine."

Young Man:
"How beautiful you are, my beloved, how beautiful!
Your eyes are soft like doves."

Young Woman:
"What a lovely, pleasant sight you are, my love, as we lie
here on the grass, shaded by cedar trees
and spreading firs."

SONG OF SONGS 1:1–2, 15–17 (NLT)

EVELYN DE MORGAN
FLORA

· A BEAUTIFUL BRIDE ·

How beautiful you are, my beloved, how beautiful! Your eyes behind your veil are like doves. Your hair falls in waves, like flocks of goats frisking across the slopes of Gilead.

Your lips are like a ribbon of scarlet. Oh, how beautiful your mouth! Your neck is as stately as the tower of David, jeweled with the shields of a thousand heroes. Your breasts are like twin fawns of a gazelle, feeding among the lilies.

You are so beautiful, my beloved, so perfect in every part. You have ravished my heart, my treasure, my bride.

SONG OF SONGS 4:1, 3–5, 9 (NLT)

CLAUDE MONET
A WOMAN READING

· A PRIVATE GARDEN ·

How sweet is your love, my treasure, my bride! How much better it is than wine! Your perfume is more fragrant than the richest of spices.

Your lips, my bride, are as sweet as honey. Yes, honey and cream are under your tongue. The scent of your clothing is like that of the mountains and the cedars of Lebanon.

You are like a private garden, my treasure, my bride! You are like a spring that no one else can drink from, a fountain of my own. You are like a lovely orchard bearing precious fruit, with the rarest of perfumes: nard and saffron, calamus and cinnamon, myrrh and aloes, perfume from every incense tree, and every other lovely spice.

You are a garden fountain, a well of living water, as refreshing as the streams from the Lebanon mountains.

SONG OF SONGS 4:10–15 (NLT)

EDMOND VERSTRAETEN
PAINTER WITH HIS MODEL

· LOVE'S PASSION ·

I am my lover's, the one he desires.
Come, my love, let us go out into the fields and
spend the night among the wildflowers.

Let us get up early and go out to the vineyards. Let us see
whether the vines have budded, whether the blossoms have
opened, and whether the pomegranates are in flower.
And there I will give you my love.

There the mandrakes give forth their fragrance, and the
rarest fruits are at our doors, the new as well as old, for
I have stored them up for you, my lover.

SONG OF SONGS 7:10–13 (NLT)

LEONARDO DA VINCI
HEAD OF WILD YOUNG GIRL (LEDA)

· THE FLAME OF LOVE ·

Young Woman:
"Place me like a seal over your heart, or like a seal on your arm. For love is as strong as death, and its jealousy is as enduring as the grave. Love flashes like fire, the brightest kind of flame.

Many waters cannot quench love; neither can rivers drown it. If a man tried to buy love with everything he owned, his offer would be utterly despised."

Young Man:
"O my beloved, lingering in the gardens, how wonderful that your companions can listen to your voice.
Let me hear it, too!"

Young Woman:
"Come quickly, my love! Move like a swift gazelle or a young deer on the
mountains of spices."

SONG OF SONGS 8:6–7, 13–14 (NLT)

A LIFE OF CONTENTMENT

WHERE THE SOUL IS
FULL OF PEACE AND JOY,
OUTWARD SURROUNDINGS
AND CIRCUMSTANCES
ARE OF COMPARATIVELY
LITTLE ACCOUNT.

Hannah Whithall Smith

CAMILLE PISSARRO
CHURCH AND FARM OF ERAGNY

PIERRE-AUGUSTE RENOIR
DANCE IN THE CITY

· BEGINNING LIFE TOGETHER ·

~◯)(◯~

Unless the LORD builds the house,
its builders labor in vain.

Unless the LORD watches over the city,
the watchmen stand guard in vain.

In vain you rise early
and stay up late,
toiling for food to eat—
for he grants sleep to those he loves.

Let your fountain be blessed,
And rejoice with the wife of your youth,
And always be enraptured with her love.

PSALMS 127:1–2 (NIV); PROVERBS 5:18, 19 (NKJV)

ROBERT REID
DAYLILIES

· DON'T WORRY ·

ook at the birds in the air. They don't plant or harvest or store food in barns, but your heavenly Father feeds them. And you know that you are worth much more than the birds.

And why do you worry about clothes? Look at how the lilies in the field grow. They don't work or make clothes for themselves. But I tell you that even Solomon with his riches was not dressed as beautifully as one of these flowers.

Don't worry and say, "What will we eat?" or "What will we drink?" or "What will we wear?"

The thing you should want most is God's kingdom and doing what God wants. Then all these other things you need will be given to you.

MATTHEW 6:26, 28–29, 31, 33 (NCV)

JEAN-HONORÉ FRAGONARD
YOUNG GIRL READING

· HONOR THE LORD ·

Trust in the LORD with all your heart; do not depend on your own understanding.

Seek his will in all you do, and he will direct your paths.

Don't be impressed with your own wisdom. Instead, fear the LORD and turn your back on evil.

Then you will gain renewed health and vitality.

Honor the LORD with your wealth and with the best part of everything your land produces.

Then he will fill your barns with grain, and your vats will overflow with the finest wine.

PROVERBS 3:5–10 (NLT)

CLAUDE MONET
THE LUNCHEON: MONET'S GARDEN AT ARGENTEUIL

· AN OPEN HOME ·

Continue to love each other with true
Christian love.

Don't forget to show hospitality
to strangers, for some who have done this have entertained
angels without realizing it!

When you give a luncheon or dinner, do not invite your
friends, your brothers or relatives, or your rich neighbors; if
you do, they may invite you back and so you will be repaid.

But when you give a banquet, invite the poor, the crippled,
the lame, the blind,
and you will be blessed. Although they cannot repay you,
you will be repaid at the resurrection of the righteous.

HEBREWS 13:1–2 (NLT); LUKE 14:12–14 (NIV)

MARY CASSATT
MOTHER AND CHILD

· TRUE CONTENTMENT ·

Keep your lives free from the love of money and be content with what you have, because God has said,

> "Never will I leave you;
> Never will I forsake you."

Yet true religion with contentment is great wealth. After all, we didn't bring anything with us when we came into the world, and we certainly cannot carry anything with us when we die. So if we have enough food and clothing, let us be content.

For the love of money is at the root of all kinds of evil.

HEBREWS 13:5 (NIV); 1 TIMOTHY 6:6–8, 10 (NLT)

ARTHUR HUGHES
THE LONG ENGAGEMENT

· A HIGH CALLING ·

Lead a life worthy of your calling, for you have been called by God.

Be humble and gentle. Be patient with each other, making allowance for each other's faults because of your love.

Always keep yourselves united in the Holy Spirit, and bind yourselves together with peace.

We are all one body, we have the same Spirit, and we have all been called to the same glorious future. There is only one Lord, one faith, one baptism, and there is only one God and Father, who is over us all and in us all and living through us all.

EPHESIANS 4:1–6 (NLT)

ANGELO MORBELLI
DREAM AND REALITY

· LISTENING HEARTS ·

Everyone should be quick to listen, slow to speak and slow to become angry, for man's anger does not bring about the righteous life that God desires.

"In your anger do not sin":
Do not let the sun go down while you are still angry,
and do not give the devil a foothold.

A gentle answer turns away wrath, but a harsh word
stirs up anger.

JAMES 1:19–20; EPHESIANS 4:26–27; PROVERBS 15:1 (NIV)

CHILDREN

CHILDREN ARE NOT OUR
PROPERTIES TO OWN OR
RULE OVER, BUT GIFTS TO
CHERISH AND CARE FOR.
OUR CHILDREN ARE OUR
MOST IMPORTANT
GUESTS, WHO ENTER
INTO OUR HOME, ASK
FOR CAREFUL ATTENTION,
STAY FOR A WHILE, AND
THEN LEAVE TO FOLLOW
THEIR OWN WAY.

Henri Nouwen

MARY CASSATT
WOMAN AND CHILDREN

FREDERICK MORGAN
GOING TO THE FAIR

· A GODLY HERITAGE ·

Behold, children are a heritage from the LORD, the fruit of the womb is a reward.

Like arrows in the hand of a warrior, so are the children of one's youth.

Grandchildren are the crown of the aged, and the glory of children is their parents.

If anyone does not provide for his relatives, and especially for his immediate family, he has denied the faith and is worse than an unbeliever.

PSALMS 127:3–4 (NKJV); PROVERBS 17:6 (NRSV); 1 TIMOTHY 5:8 (NIV)

JAMES CHARLES
THE PICNIC

· TRUE HAPPINESS ·

ow happy are those who fear the LORD–
all who follow his ways!

You will enjoy the fruit of your labor.
How happy you will be! How rich your life!

Your wife will be like a fruitful vine,
flourishing within your home.
And look at all those children!
There they sit around your table
as vigorous and healthy as young olive trees.

That is the LORD's reward
for those who fear him.

PSALMS 128:1–4 (NLT)

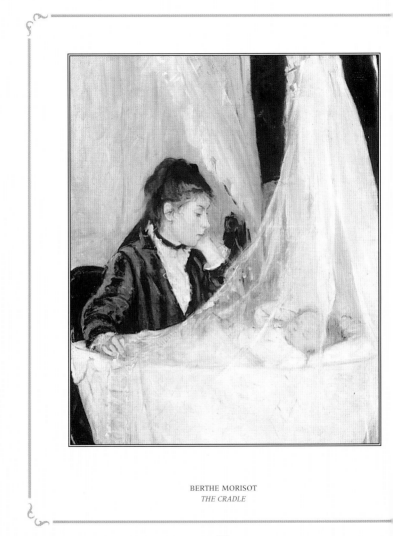

BERTHE MORISOT
THE CRADLE

· A MOTHER'S LOVE ·

Hannah was in deep anguish, crying bitterly as she prayed to the LORD.

And she made this vow:
"O LORD Almighty, if you will look down upon my sorrow
and answer my prayer and give me a son, then I will
give him back to you."

In due time she gave birth to a son. She named
him Samuel, for she said,
"I asked the LORD for him."

Then Hannah prayed:
"My heart rejoices in the LORD!
Oh, how the LORD has blessed me!
No one is holy like the LORD!
There is no one besides you;
there is no Rock like our God."

1 SAMUEL 1:10–11, 20; 2:1, 2 (NLT)

JEAN-BAPTISTE SIMÉON CHARDIN
THE YOUNG SCHOOL MISTRESS

· RAISING CHILDREN ·

rain up a child in the way he should go: and when
he is old, he will not depart from it.

You must love the LORD your God with all your heart,
all your soul, and all your strength.

And you must commit yourselves wholeheartedly to these
commands I am giving you today.

Repeat them again and again to your children. Talk about
them when you are at home and when you are away on a
journey, when you are lying down and when you
are getting up again.

If you refuse to discipline your children, it proves you don't
love them; if you love your children, you will be prompt
to discipline them.

The godly walk with integrity; blessed are their children
after them.

PROVERBS 22:6 (KJV); DEUTERONOMY 6:5–7 (NLT);
PROVERBS 13:24, 20:7 (NLT)

PIERRE-AUGUSTE RENOIR
GABRIELLE AND JEAN

· A SPIRITUAL LEGACY ·

We will tell the next generation about the Lord's power and great deeds and the miraculous things he has done.

He established written instructions for Jacob's people. He gave his teachings to Israel. He commanded our ancestors to make them known to their children so that the next generation would know them.

Children yet to be born would learn them. They will grow up and tell their children to trust God, to remember what he has done, and to obey his commands.

PSALMS 78:4–7 (GWT)

THOMAS GAINSBOROUGH
THE PAINTERS DAUGHTERS CHASING A BUTTERFLY

· CHILDLIKE FAITH ·

〜)(〜

eople were bringing little children to him in order
that he might touch them; and the disciples spoke
sternly to them.

But when Jesus saw this, he was indignant and
said to them,

"Let the little children come to me; do not stop them; for
it is to such as these that the kingdom of God belongs.

"Truly I tell you, whoever does not receive the kingdom of
God as a little child will never enter it." And he took them
up in his arms, laid his hands on them, and blessed them.

MARK 10:13–16 (NRSV)

LIVING A GODLY LIFE

LORD, GIVE ME AN
OPEN HEART TO FIND
YOU EVERYWHERE, TO
GLIMPSE THE HEAVEN
ENFOLDED IN A BUD,
AND TO EXPERIENCE
ETERNITY IN THE
SMALLEST ACT OF LOVE.

Mother Teresa

JOHN CONSTABLE
WIVENHOE PARK, ESSEX

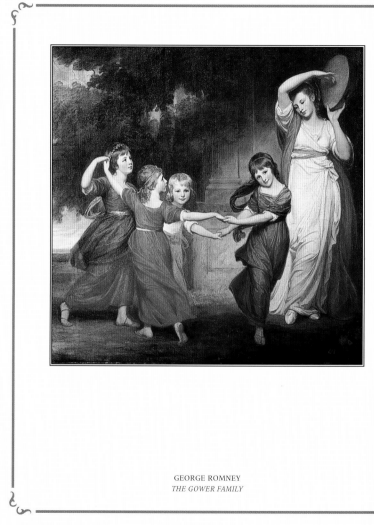

GEORGE ROMNEY
THE GOWER FAMILY

· GENUINE LOVE ·

I give you a new command: Love each other. You must love each other as I have loved you.

All people will know that you are my followers if you love each other.

Better is a dinner of herbs where love is, than a fatted calf with hatred.

Be kind to each other, tenderhearted, forgiving one another, just as God through Christ has forgiven you.

JOHN 13:34–35 (NCV); PROVERBS 15:17 (NKJV); EPHESIANS 4:32 (NLT)

JESSICA HAYLLAR
FRESH FROM THE ALTAR

· LIVE IN LOVE ·

The fruit of the Spirit is love, joy, peace, patience, kindness, goodness, faithfulness, gentleness, and self-control. Against such things there is no law.

Let all that you do be done in love.

Continue to show deep love for each other,
for love covers a multitude of sins.

If we love each other, God lives in us, and his love has
been brought to full expression through us.

GALATIANS 5:22–23 (NIV); 1 CORINTHIANS 16:14 (NASB); 1 PETER 4:8;
1 JOHN 4:12 (NLT)

PIERRE-AUGUSTE RENOIR
A DANCE IN THE COUNTRY

· PERFECT UNITY ·

I pray that your love for each other will overflow more and more, and that you will keep on growing in your knowledge and understanding.

For I want you to understand what really matters, so that you may live pure and blameless lives until Christ returns.

Therefore, as God's chosen people, holy and dearly loved, clothe yourselves with compassion, kindness, humility, gentleness and patience.

Bear with each other and forgive whatever grievances you may have against one another. Forgive as the Lord forgave you.

And over all these virtues put on love, which binds them all together in perfect unity.

PHILIPPIANS 1:9–10 (NLT); COLOSSIANS 3:12–14 (NIV)

PIERRE-AUGUSTE RENOIR
BEACH SCENE, GUERNSEY

· LIVE IN HARMONY ·

Let love be genuine; hate what is evil, hold fast to what is good; love one another with mutual affection; outdo one another in showing honor.

Do not lag in zeal, be ardent in spirit, serve the Lord.
Rejoice in hope, be patient in suffering, persevere in prayer.
Contribute to the needs of the saints; extend
hospitality to strangers.
Bless those who persecute you; bless and
do not curse them.
Rejoice with those who rejoice, weep with those who weep.

Live in harmony with one another; do not be haughty, but
associate with the lowly; do not claim to be wiser
than you are. Do not repay anyone evil for evil, but
take thought for what is noble in the sight of all. If it is
possible, so far as it depends on you, live
peaceably with all.

ROMANS 12:9–18 (NRSV)

SIR GEORGE CLAUSEN
FRENCH PEASANT GIRLS PRAYING

· WISDOM FROM GOD ·

But the wisdom that comes from heaven is first of all pure; then peace-loving, considerate, submissive, full of mercy and good fruit, impartial, and sincere.

Peacemakers who sow in peace raise a harvest of righteousness.

But also for this very reason, giving all diligence, add to your faith virtue, to virtue knowledge, to knowledge self-control, to self-control perseverance, to perseverance godliness, to godliness brotherly kindness, and to brotherly kindness love.

For if these things are yours and abound, you will be neither barren nor unfruitful in the knowledge of our Lord Jesus Christ.

JAMES 3:17–18 (NIV); 2 PETER 1:5–8 (NKJV)

MARY LOUISE MACMONNIES
ROSES AND LILIES

· WALKING IN THE LIGHT ·

f we walk in the light as He Himself is in the light, we have fellowship with one another, and the blood of Jesus His Son cleanses us from all sin.

If we say that we have no sin, we are deceiving ourselves, and the truth is not in us.

If we confess our sins, He is faithful and righteous to forgive us our sins and to cleanse us from all unrighteousness.

Dear children, let us stop saying we love each other; let us really show it by our actions. It is by our actions that we know we are living in the truth.

Beloved, let us love one another, for love is from God; and everyone who loves is born of God and knows God.

1 JOHN 1:7–9 (NASB); 3:18–19 (NLT); 4:7 (NASB)

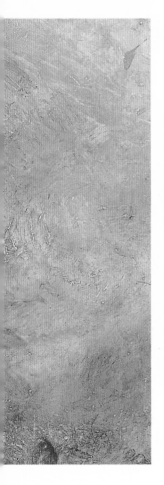

FACING LIFE'S DIFFICULTIES

HAVE CONFIDENCE IN
GOD'S MERCY, FOR WHEN
YOU THINK HE IS A LONG
WAY FROM YOU, HE
IS OFTEN QUITE NEAR.

Thomas à Kempis

J.M.W. TURNER
ANGEL STANDING IN STORM

85

WILLIAM HOLMAN HUNT
OUR ENGLISH COASTS

· BESIDE STILL WATERS ·

The LORD is my shepherd; I shall not want.

He maketh me to lie down in green pastures: he leadeth me beside the still waters.

He restoreth my soul: he leadeth me in the paths of righteousness for his name's sake.

Yea, though I walk through the valley of the shadow of death, I will fear no evil: for thou art with me; thy rod and thy staff they comfort me.

Thou preparest a table before me in the presence of mine enemies: thou anointest my head with oil; my cup runneth over.

Surely goodness and mercy shall follow me all the days of my life: and I will dwell in the house of the LORD for ever.

PSALMS 23:1–6 (KJV)

BOSSANYI
WINDOW OF SALVATION

· DIVINE PROTECTION ·

G od is our protection and our strength. He always helps in times of trouble.

So we will not be afraid even if the earth shakes, or the mountains fall into the sea, even if the oceans roar and foam, or the mountains shake at the raging sea.

"Do not fear, for I am with you; do not anxiously look about you, for I am your God. I will strengthen you, surely I will help you, surely I will uphold you with My righteous right hand."

But they that wait upon the LORD shall renew their strength; they shall mount up with wings as eagles; they shall run, and not be weary; and they shall walk, and not faint.

PSALMS 46:1–3 (NCV); ISAIAH 41:10 (NASB), 40:31 (KJV)

RUBENS
STUDY OF THE HEAD OF ST. APOLLONIA

· FULL OF HOPE ·

Are not two sparrows sold for a penny? Yet not one of them will fall to the ground apart from the will of your Father.

And even the very hairs of your head are
all numbered.

So don't be afraid; you are worth more
than many sparrows.

For I am persuaded that neither death nor life, nor angels
nor principalities nor powers, nor things present
nor things to come,
nor height nor depth, nor any other created thing, shall be
able to separate us from the love of God which is in
Christ Jesus our Lord.

Be joyful because you have hope. Be patient when trouble
comes, and pray at all times.

MATTHEW 10:29–31 (NIV); ROMANS 8:38–39 (NKJV), 12:12 (NCV)

JEAN-BAPTISTE SIMÉON CHARDIN
SAYING GRACE

· DAILY COMFORT ·

All praise to the God and Father of our Lord Jesus Christ. He is the source of every mercy and the God who comforts us.

He comforts us in all our troubles so that we can comfort others.

Give all your worries and cares to God, for he cares about what happens to you.

And my God will supply all your needs according to His riches in glory in Christ Jesus.

In the multitude of my anxieties within me, your comforts delight my soul.

2 CORINTHIANS 1:3–4 (NLT); 1 PETER 5:7 (NLT); PHILIPPIANS 4:19 (NASB);
PSALMS 94:19 (NKJV)

· THE WEDDING PARTY ·

Mother of the bride

Father of the bride

Mother of the groom

Father of the groom

Bride's attendants

Groom's attendants

· THE WEDDING SERVICE ·

⌒)(⌒

The place

_____

The Minister

_____

Music played at the wedding

_____

Recording of your wedding vows

_____

_____

_____

· ACKNOWLEDGMENTS ·

The publisher would like to thank the following for their kind permission to reproduce their photographs:

AKG London: National Gallery of Art, Washington, 68-69 Bridgeman Art Library, London/New York: 40/A & F Pears Ltd., London, UK, 20/Birmingham Museums and Art Gallery, 50/Bulloz, Paris, France, 46/Christie's Images, 22, 70/courtesy of the artist's estate/Christie's Images 72/City of Bristol Museum and Art Gallery, UK 16, 18/Galleria degli Uffizi, Florence, Italy 88/Louvre, Paris, France/Giraudon 90/Magyar Nemzeti Galeria, Budapest, Hungary 26/The de Morgan Foundation, London, UK 30/Musee d'Orsay, Paris 74/Musee d'Orsay, Paris/Giraudon 38-39/Musee d'Orsay, Paris, France/Peter Willi 60/Musee d'Orsay, Paris, France/Bulloz 40/Musee l'Orangerie, Paris, France/Bulloz 64/Musee des Beaux Arts, Rouen, France/Giraudon 6-7/Musee des Beaux Arts, Rouen, France/Giraudon 80/National Gallery of Art, Washington, DC, USA 44 /National Gallery of Scotland, Edinburgh, UK 24 - 25/National Gallery, London, UK 12, 62, 66/Osterreichische Galerie, Vienna, Austria 28/Phillips, The International Fine Art Auctioneers, UK 14/Private Collection 10/Private Collection/Giraudon 48/Roy Miles Gallery, London, UK 56 / Victoria & Albert Museum, London, UK 78/Walters Art Gallery, Baltimore, Maryland, USA/Giraudon 32/Warrington Museum & Art Gallery, Cheshire, UK 58 Dean and Chapter of Canterbury: 86 by courtesy of the Fogg Art Museum, Harvard University Art Museum, gift of Dr Ernest G Stillman: 54-55 Rijksmuseum, Amsterdam: 8 SuperStock: Barnes Foundation, Merion, Pennsylvania, USA 76/Casa di Risparmio della Provincia Lombarda/Fratelli Alinari 52/Christie's Images 42/National Gallery, Parma, Italy/Giraudon, Paris, France, 36/Private collection 34 Tate Gallery Publishing: 82, 84.